AMSTERDAM

THE CITY AT A GLANCE

GU00836273

Westerkerk
From its 85m tower, the 'Western
impressive views over gallery-ri
Prinsengracht 281, T 624 7766

Stadsschouwburg
This neo-Renaissance theatre is at the
heart of nightlife square Leidseplein.
See p037

Centraal Station
Amsterdam boasts this majestic 19th-century
railway terminal as its main transport hub.
Stationsplein

Van Gogh Museum
On show in the main building is the artist's
work; temporary exhibitions are housed in
Kisho Kurokawa's 1999 extension.
See p014

Rijksmuseum
Dating from 1885, this museum is where the
nation's Golden Age treasures are displayed.
See p032

Stadsarchief
Designed by Dutch architect KPC de Bazel,
the municipal archive is a monumental
example of polychromatic brickwork.
See p010

NEMO
Renzo Piano's ship-like science centre
sits on top of the cars-only IJtunnel, the
city's underwater connection to Noord.
See p012

Hermitage Amsterdam
This branch of the St Petersburg museum
has made its mark as a local arts institution.
See p035

INTRODUCTION

THE CHANGING FACE OF THE URBAN SCENE

Defeating the shifting sands of time, Amsterdam – like Venice – is a grand, architectural marvel that sits on a warren of ancient canals. Unlike its Italian counterpart, however, it is an evolving metropolis and not a bejewelled museum piece. A glimpse into the uncurtained windows of the 17th-century canal-houses lining its four principal waterways speaks volumes about the city's psyche. Often modernised and always welcoming, these interiors reveal an artistic, mercantile people with an irreverent sense of humour; qualities also seen in the work of the Dutch designers who took the world by storm at the start of the millennium.

Ever wily to the winds of change, Amsterdam has picked up on the success of Marcel Wanders, Hella Jongerius and the progeny of Droog by producing a string of new hotels, restaurants, bars and clubs to meet the modern needs of its many visitors. And to accommodate the swelling number of inhabitants, a brave new world of futuristic developments has emerged from reclaimed land in the eastern docklands, and even further out at IJburg.

Meanwhile, local government has been striving to tame the beasts – sex, drugs and rock 'n' roll – that have made Amsterdam infamous. The red-light district, in particular, has been getting a clean-up, with the number of coffeeshops (victims of the smoking ban) and neon-framed windows beginning to decline slowly, as high-end restaurants, shops and design studios enter the mix.

ESSENTIAL INFO
FACTS, FIGURES AND USEFUL ADDRESSES

TOURIST OFFICE
Stationsplein 10
T 201 8800
www.iamsterdam.com

TRANSPORT
Bicycle hire
MacBike
T 624 8391
www.macbike.nl
Car hire
Avis
T 088 284 7000
Taxis
Taxicentrale
T 777 7777
Watertaxi
T 535 6363
Hailing taxis in the street is difficult, but ranks are plentiful in the city centre, or you can book a cab in advance

EMERGENCY SERVICES
Central Medical Service (24 hours)
T 592 3434
Emergencies
T 112
Late-night pharmacy
Apotheek Leidsestraat
Leidsestraat 74-76
T 422 0210
da-apotheekleidsestraat.apotheek.org

CONSULATES
British Consulate
Koningslaan 44
T 676 4343
www.ukinnl.fco.gov.uk
US Consulate
Museumplein 19
T 575 5309
amsterdam.usconsulate.gov

POSTAL SERVICES
Post office
Singel 250
T 090 0767 8526
Shipping
UPS
T 090 0225 5877

BOOKS
Amsterdam: A Traveler's Literary Companion edited by Manfred Wolf (Whereabouts Press)
Dutch Design: A History by Mienke Simon Thomas (Reaktion Books)
Amsterdam: The Brief Life of a City by Geert Mak (Vintage)

WEBSITES
Art/Design
www.stedelijk.nl
www.design.nl
Newspaper
www.nrc.nl

EVENTS
Amsterdam Fashion Week
www.amsterdamfashionweek.com
Art Amsterdam
www.artamsterdam.nl

COST OF LIVING
Taxi from Amsterdam Schiphol Airport to city centre
€40
Cappuccino
€3
Packet of cigarettes
€5
Daily newspaper
€2
Bottle of champagne
€80

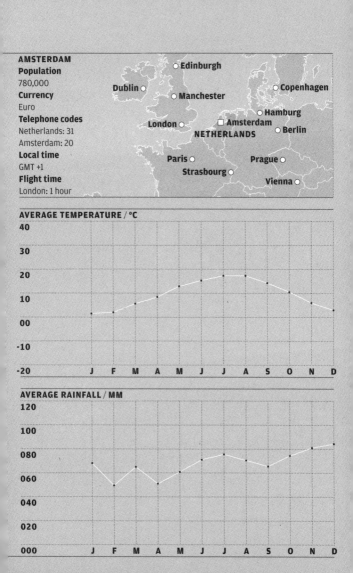

AMSTERDAM
Population
780,000
Currency
Euro
Telephone codes
Netherlands: 31
Amsterdam: 20
Local time
GMT +1
Flight time
London: 1 hour

Edinburgh
Dublin ○
Copenhagen
Manchester
Hamburg
London ○   □ Amsterdam   Berlin
NETHERLANDS
Paris ○   Prague ○
Strasbourg ○
Vienna ○

AVERAGE TEMPERATURE / °C

	J	F	M	A	M	J	J	A	S	O	N	D
40												
30												
20												
10												
00												
-10												
-20												

AVERAGE RAINFALL / MM

	J	F	M	A	M	J	J	A	S	O	N	D
120												
100												
080												
060												
040												
020												
000												

NEIGHBOURHOODS

THE AREAS YOU NEED TO KNOW AND WHY

To help you navigate the city, we've chosen the most interesting districts (see below and the map inside the back cover) and colour-coded our featured venues, according to their location; those venues that are outside these areas are not coloured.

DE PIJP

This southern suburb claims to be the most multicultural in Europe. Ever since its student and artistic residents were joined by expats and media types, the area has become extremely happening. De Pijp's daily Albert Cuypmarkt and the laidback Brasserie Witteveen (Ceintuurbaan 256-260, T 344 6406) are local institutions. Head south to admire the housing around Henriette Ronnerplein, which was built in the style of the Amsterdam School.

WESTERPARK

In 2003, when the 19th-century gasworks of Westergasfabriek (Polonceaukade 27, T 586 0710) was converted into a buzzy arts complex, complete with galleries, a cinema, a bar, a theatre and restaurants, the fortunes of this former working-class district began to improve. In the elegant Westerpark itself, locals come to unwind in its cafés, stroll, jog and play tennis.

CENTRUM

Amsterdam's notorious red-light district, where brothels are gradually being replaced by design studios, is located in the heart of the city, and is ringed by the 17th-century canals Singel, Herengracht, Keizersgracht and Prinsengracht. The area is crowned by the stately Centraal Station, the capital's impressive neo-Renaissance gateway. Centrum is also the prime shopping zone; don't miss the iconic design collective Droog (see p082).

JORDAAN

When the city's aristocracy constructed their elegant canal houses in the 17th century, they also built the Jordaan to house craftsmen, brewers, tanners and merchants, and to keep them on the other side of Prinsengracht. For centuries, Jordaaners formed a tight community, but the area's charming streets, such as Brouwersgracht, are now the stomping ground of the hip thirtysomethings who frequent the bars and restaurants.

HAVENS OOST

The manmade islands of KNSM and Java, and the Borneo Sporenburg peninsula, began life as humble wave breaks and then housed shipping company offices and warehouses. Today, innovative architecture and state-of-the-art housing, such as the impressive bulk of The Whale (see p013), appeal to young families, and the area has become highly desirable.

OUD ZUID

At the end of the 19th century, Amsterdam expanded rapidly, with Oud Zuid becoming an important new district. The landscaped green space of Vondelpark prompted the construction of many a mansion, and the cultural playground that is Museumplein now draws art lovers in their droves. Popular attractions here include the Van Gogh Museum (see p014), the stately Rijksmuseum (see p032), and the Stedelijk Museum (see p032), revamped in 2012.

LANDMARKS

THE SHAPE OF THE CITY SKYLINE

Visitors to Amsterdam often long to stay and make it their home. It has everything that you could want from a city, including a compact layout that's just right for aimless strolling, and above all, it offers a simple civic lesson: raise tolerance to the level of principle and, after a time, there will be little need to exercise it.

As with most other northern European cities, Amsterdam is predicated on the need and desire to be tucked up at home for a good chunk of the year. At the same time, its interiors always seem to be on display to the outside world, and one of its pleasures is not just window-shopping, but window *living*. What must it be like to live in those high-ceilinged apartments on Prinsengracht, with their exquisite lights and minimal decor? Or to gaze out at the canals, which, here and there, reflect the lights hung under the bridges to form magical, sparkling yellow necklaces? All of which is to say that Amsterdam's charms are discreet ones.

This is one of the world's great walking cities, but, unlike in New York or Paris, the way here is seldom marked by the narcissistic tower block or the dominating civic structure. If you want to relieve your eyes from the gorgeous claustrophobia of the canals, head out to KNSM-eiland, the squeaky-clean eastern dockside development that has taken the concept of a quaint Amsterdam architectural vernacular and blown it right out of the water. *For full addresses, see Resources.*

Stadsarchief
Known as De Bazel after its architect,
this former investment-bank HQ,
completed in 1926, is home to the reams
of historic maps, files and drawings that
make up the municipal archive. The
facade is a showpiece of 20th-century
Dutch architecture, whereas inside are
art deco murals, stained-glass artworks
and monumental period rooms.
Vijzelstraat 32, T 251 1510

NEMO

The roof of Renzo Piano's ship-like science museum is conceived as a city square, the modern equivalent of the elegant spaces found in the historic centre. It's just about the only raised public area in this famously flat city, and, offering a good view back to old Amsterdam, draws considerable summer crowds. In spirit, the building, which is surrounded by water on three sides, echoes the massive Borneo Sporenburg dockland area, where much of the city's boldest architecture is concentrated. When it opened in 1997 it was dismissed by local architects as 'half a Renzo Piano' building, because they felt corners had been cut on the finish and choice of materials in order to hit a notoriously tight budget. Gradually, though, it's come to be loved by locals.
Oosterdok 2, T 531 3233, www.e-nemo.nl

The Whale

Even among the multitude of modern buildings that comprise the Sporenburg peninsula redevelopment project, this housing complex stands out. The size of a football stadium, it squats in the former harbour just like a beached whale, hence its name, and is suitably grey in colour. Completed in 2000 by architects Cie, and one of only three large-scale structures in an area where low-rises predominate,

The Whale is an incredibly sophisticated mixed-use development. The roof is angled to elevate the building on two sides and maximise sunlight in the apartments within. The complex sometimes hosts cultural events.
Baron GA Tindalplein, Borneo Sporenburg

Van Gogh Museum

The Japanese architect Kisho Kurokawa had a tough act to follow when he was asked to design the Van Gogh Museum's exhibition wing: the main building is an understated modern classic designed in the early 1960s by Gerrit Rietveld, a leading light in the celebrated De Stijl group. Yet Kurokawa's contribution, completed in 1999, is actually more of a crowd-pleaser than Rietveld's – the highlight of the cultural grand prix that is the Museumplein. A visit during late-night opening on Fridays (until 10pm) is a good way to avoid the crowds. The Van Gogh Museum reopens after a seven-month renovation in May 2013; before this date, some of the collection will be shown at the Hermitage Amsterdam (see p035). *Paulus Potterstraat 7, T 570 5200, www.vangoghmuseum.nl*

HOTELS

WHERE TO STAY AND WHICH ROOMS TO BOOK

Just like Paris and Barcelona, Amsterdam is a classic mini-break destination, but its relatively small size means the city's hotels are often booked up, especially from March until mid-September. Up until the 1990s, accommodation here was restricted to grotty flophouses, mid-range corporate monoliths, and grandes dames, such as Amstel (Professor Tulpplein 1, T 622 6060), The Grand (Oudezijds Voorburgwal 197, T 555 3111) and the Hotel de l'Europe (Nieuwe Doelenstraat 2-14, T 531 1777), renovated in 2010.

The 21st-century Dutch design revolution put paid to all that, however, and visitors today have a range of options. Seven One Seven (Prinsengracht 717, T 427 0717) and The College Hotel (see p026) have a refined, classic style; the Conservatorium (opposite) to the west, and Hotel Arena (see p028) and Lloyd Hotel (Oostelijke Handelskade 34, T 561 3636) in the east, attract a design-savvy crowd. The success of the latter inspired its owners to open the fashion-centric Exchange (see p024) in 2011. Amsterdam's B&Bs are also modernising fast: if the suite at Steel (see p027) is taken, try Kien (Tweede Weteringdwarsstraat 65, T 428 5262), Marcel's Creative Exchange (Leidsestraat 87, T 622 9834) or Maison Rika (Oude Spiegelstraat 12, T 330 1112), opposite the Rika boutique (see p072). Alternatively, rent out a houseboat; we liked the service at Boat For Rent Amsterdam (T 062 190 6630). *For full addresses and room rates, see Resources.*

Conservatorium Hotel

Near Museumplein, this hotel, opened in 2012, breathes with appropriately rarefied air. Located in a 19th-century building that once housed a music conservatory, the hotel features soaring ceilings, which allowed designer Piero Lissoni to renovate nearly half of the 129 rooms as duplexes (Conservatorium Suite, above). Fusing classic luxury with modernist design, interiors are a mellow mix of wood, glass and metal; some rooms preserve original pinewood beams. Public spaces include a lounge, a brasserie and Tunes Restaurant, which is focused on using local produce. However, guests seem to most appreciate the Akasha Holistic Wellbeing Center (T 570 0067; overleaf), with its glowing blue Watsu pool and hammam treatments. *Van Baerlestraat 27, T 570 0000, www.conservatoriumhotel.com*

Akasha Holistic Wellbeing Center, Conservatorium Hotel

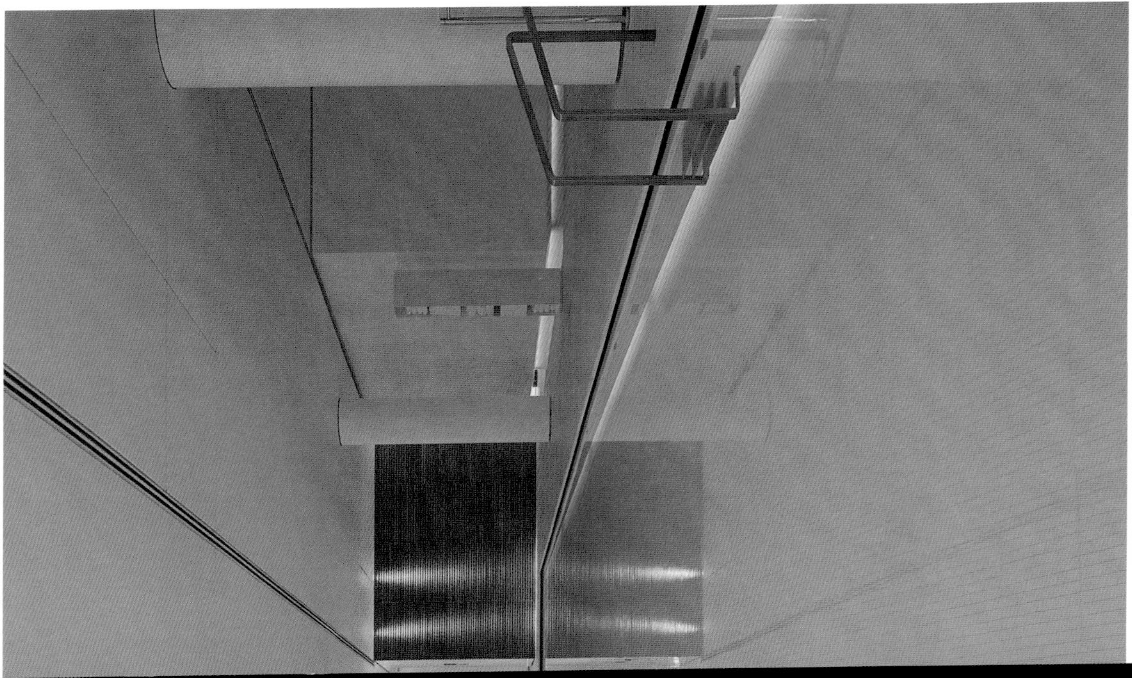

Citizen M

'Never, ever underestimate the pillow.'
That's one of the founding principles
of Concrete Architectural Associates'
prefab hotel concept, part of a wider
manifesto stating that affordability and
indulgence aren't mutually exclusive.
The rooms, the shells of which are made
in a factory off-site, have something of
the space pod about them, and come with
a touchpad that can adjust everything
from lighting to the blinds to the flat-
screen TV; the Citizen M room (above)
is standard throughout the hotel. The
homely lobby (opposite) comes saturated
with Vitra design candy that includes a
Hella Jongerius-designed 'Polder' sofa,
as well as a library of design books. For
a hotel that features an ominous-looking
automated check-in booth, there is
a reassuring number of staff on hand.
Prinses Irenestraat 30, T 811 7090,
www.citizenmamsterdamcity.com

Hotel V Frederiksplein

This successful conversion of a former stationery and office-supplies store boasts Betonlook flooring, a material that looks like concrete but doesn't crack or gather dirt. The interiors of the 48 clean-lined rooms, such as the Extra Large 211 (above), are warmed by wood panels featuring edgy graphics, and many of them are lit by Tom Dixon pendants. An international team of staff are highly engaged with the city and can point you beyond the nearby Albert Cuyp outdoor market (Albert Cuypstraat) and Utrechtsestraat shopping strip towards Amsterdam's latest arts and nightlife hotspots. The ground-floor lounge, with its fireplace and funky soul soundtrack, is a popular point from which to kickstart a night out in Centrum. *Weteringschans 136, T 662 3233, www.hotelv.nl*

The Dylan

Formerly known as Blakes, this hotel may have lost its original name but not its exquisite style. Initially designed by creator Anouska Hempel, the public spaces and rooms were revamped by local interior design firm FG Stijl in 2006, after the hotel changed hands. Today, The Dylan is furnished with reams of fabric and stacks of colour-coordinated cushions; our favourite room is the white, orchid-bedecked Loft Suite (above), which has original timber beams. In-house eateries Brasserie OCCO and Restaurant Vinkeles boast a proliferation of the black-polo-neck-and-designer-shades brigade, which creates an air of glamorous intrigue.
Keizersgracht 384, T 530 2010,
www.dylanamsterdam.com

The Exchange

After creating the Lloyd Hotel (see p016), which gained fame with its one-to-five-star rooms showcasing a veritable who's who of Dutch design, Suzanne Oxenaar and Otto Nan unveiled The Exchange, in 2011, to display the talents of the next generation of local fashion designers. Located near Centraal Station, the hotel has 61 rooms, each designed – or rather, dressed – by students of the Amsterdam Fashion Institute. The city's renowned Textielmuseum, and interior design duo Ina-Matt, acted as advisers on the beautiful yet functional spaces, which range from minimal to lush. Opt for Sofie Sleumer's Crinoline Cage Room, akin to sleeping inside a dress, or Roos Soetekouw's ruff collar-inspired Rembrandt Room New (right). Breakfast can be grabbed on site at the healthful Stock (T 427 5382). *Damrak 50, T 561 3699, www.exchangeamsterdam.com*

The College Hotel

Located minutes from Vondelpark and Museumplein, The College Hotel, which opened in 2005, takes its name from the listed 1895 school building in which it's housed. FG Stijl tastefully converted the classrooms into 40 luxurious rooms in a contemporary yet classic style, such as Deluxe Room 211 (above). The space that previously housed the gym is now a restaurant serving à la carte breakfasts, traditional Dutch dishes for lunch, and an innovative take on the local cuisine for dinner. The bar/lounge has several intimate seating areas and the poshest loos in town. The service can be patchy, as many of the staff are students from a local hotel school, although at least the educational theme is being continued. *Roelof Hartstraat 1, T 571 1511, www.thecollegehotel.com*

Steel

Designer Joris van Ingen, who collaborated with Marcel Wanders on his now-closed Lute Suites hotel, joined forces with his sister Lenneke for this single-suite B&B in the historic centre, amid an eclectic mix of restaurants, hip shops and bars, including some truly old-school hangouts. The Deluxe Apartment (above), situated on the ground floor of a characterful former warehouse, features urban necessities such as a rain shower, underfloor heating, a flat-screen television and an espresso machine. The most eye-popping element in the comfortable space is the illuminated, free-standing bath. If this isn't convincing enough, breakfast comes from Puccini (T 620 8458) across the street.
Staalstraat 32, www.staywithsteel.com

Hotel Arena

After a multimillion-euro makeover at the beginning of the new millennium and a more recent refurbishment in 2009, Arena is no longer the lowly backpack-shack full of stoned teenagers that it was in the 1980s. Today, its airy rooms, such as the Studio Room (above), attract a sophisticated clientele. Contemporary interiors and furnishings by Piet Hein Eek, Ineke Hans and Marcel Wanders complement the original features of the building, built in 1890 as an orphanage. The sleek restaurant, Todine, designed by Ronald Hooft, has a terrace and nightclub, Tonight, which is housed in the former chapel and is an institution. Grooving in the nave, when DJs from the Loveland festival take to the decks, is a must.
's-Gravesandestraat 51, T 850 2400, www.hotelarena.nl

Canal House
The renovation of this old-timer,
comprised of three 17th-century
merchants' houses, retained the best of
its past while keeping it in the present.
Ornate chimneys and timber beams now
mix with silk wallpaper, heavy velvet
curtains and modern furniture. Check
into the top-floor Best Room (pictured)
for pretty views of Keizersgracht.
Keizersgracht 148, T 622 5182

24 HOURS

SEE THE BEST OF THE CITY IN JUST ONE DAY

Amsterdam packs a mean cultural punch. The Dutch Golden Age painters and the mad, maverick Van Gogh still top the charts at the world's prestigious auction houses, and many of their most famous works hang in the city's museums. To view the Old Masters, head to Rembrandthuis (Jodenbreestraat 4, T 520 0400) and the Rijksmuseum (Jan Luijkenstraat 1, T 674 7000), which, although undergoing a facelift until mid-2013, is still showing works by Vermeer, Hals and Rembrandt in its Philips Wing.

The city's contemporary art scene is also at the cutting edge. For experimental works, visit Galerie Rademakers (Prinsengracht 570-572, T 622 5496) or W139 (Warmoesstraat 139, T 622 9434). Every spring, the historic Oude Kerk (Oudekerksplein 23, T 625 8284) is where the World Press Photo exhibition begins its global tour; the excellent photo gallery FOAM (Keizersgracht 609, T 551 6500) is also a must-see. The Stedelijk Museum (Museumplein 10, T 573 2911), which houses modern art and design, reopened in 2012 having been ambitiously expanded by Benthem Crouwel Architects; in the same year, the EYE Film Institute (see p065), launched on the northern bank of the IJ River. Of course, no trip to Amsterdam would be complete without a tour of those 17th-century canals, which can be explored by bicycle (MacBike; see p088) or preferably from the water (www.water-taxi.nl).
For full addresses, see Resources.

09.30 Vlaamsch Broodhuys

A fragrant haven of savoury delicacies and sweet pastries, Vlaamsch Broodhuys' MO is sourdough bread, baked using *camp rémy*, the grand cru of wheat flour. Owner and baker Dimitri Roels' artisanal approach lures a loyal crowd, especially for the hefty 2kg *pains grand-mères*; less gargantuan goodies include open sandwiches and Burgundian pastries, alongside fresh juice and coffee. On warm days, the outdoor seats can fill up quickly, although there's something to be said for sitting inside too, where the rawness of the high-ceilinged industrial space has been softened by simple wooden tables and white-painted chairs. In addition to this branch, a stone's throw from the Vondelpark, there are three more in town. *Eerste Constantijn Huygensstraat 64, T 689 9131, www.vlaamschbroodhuys.nl*

11.00 Moooi

In Moooi – the Dutch word for 'beautiful' but with an extra 'o' – Marcel Wanders and Casper Vissers have created a gallery-cum-shop that showcases some of the country's hottest design upstarts. The 700 sq m showroom has been a favourite haunt for artists, professionals and students since its 2008 opening, marking the final stage of the transformation of the Jordaan from a working-class district into one of Amsterdam's trendiest areas. Alongside the innovative lighting that is Moooi's trademark, design books and a range of gadgets means there are also plenty of hand luggage-friendly finds on sale. A 2011 revamp added dozens of new designs, further establishing this space as a showcase for the international brand. *Westerstraat 187, T 528 7760, www.moooi.com*

12.30 Hermitage Amsterdam

In a building that was once a refuge for elderly women, this outpost of the St Petersburg museum reopened in 2009 following a €40m renovation. The simple, luminous space, which has a massive inner courtyard, embraces the new while managing to preserve elements of the building's late-17th-century Dutch heritage. Biannual exhibitions span the realms of international art, archaeology and history, and a permanent collection details the historical relationship between Russia and the Netherlands. A highly regarded restaurant, Neva (T 530 7483), led by chef Ricardo van Ede, overlooks the courtyard gardens. Next door, where the museum used to be, is now the location of its Hermitage for Children, a cultural facility for Amsterdam's young.
Amstel 51, T 530 7488, www.hermitage.nl

15.00 Rabozaal

With its burger giants and chain pubs, it can be tempting to cross the tourist-trap Leidseplein area off one's list altogether. But to do so would be to miss out on two of the most delightful and innovative arts venues Amsterdam has to offer: dance and drama theatre Stadsschouwburg (T 624 2311) – which also has an excellent café – and its hipper, gig-loving neighbour Melkweg (T 531 8181), whose name translates as 'milky way'. In-between the two, Rabozaal juts from the side of the former and overhangs the latter. A bank-sponsored joint venture for live music, it features adaptable seating and state-of-the-art sound design. Although it's certainly one of the city's most technically advanced propositions, it is also a surprisingly intimate performance space. *Leidseplein 26, T 624 2311, www.ssba.nl*

19.30 De Kas

Deep in east Amsterdam, this 1926 greenhouse now houses a restaurant that, since opening in 2001, has steadily become the city's forerunner of all that is locally grown and sourced. The daily Mediterranean-inspired set menus are based around fresh vegetables and herbs harvested at sunrise in an adjoining garden and nearby nursery, by founder and owner Gert Jan Hageman. These ingredients are then matched with the best of what De Kas' organic meat and fish suppliers have to offer, delivering dishes such as grilled sea bass or lamb chop served with a salad of edible flowers, and crusty potato pie. Lunch is available on weekdays only, and in summer can be taken on the patio of the herb garden. *Kamerlingh Onneslaan 3, T 462 4562, www.restaurantdekas.nl*

URBAN LIFE
CAFÉS, RESTAURANTS, BARS AND NIGHTCLUBS

The dining scene in Amsterdam is a seasonal affair. Once the bulbs have bloomed in May, the *nieuwe haring* (new herring) season begins and locals indulge in their answer to sashimi – garnished with onion and gherkin and bought from street stalls. The streets lining the canals evoke a Continental café scene between midday and midnight, when open sandwiches washed down with *witbier* are an essential. At the height of summer, hipsters swarm to the (very) urban beaches Amsterdam Roest (Czaar Peterstraat 213, T 308 0283) and Hannekes Boom (Dijksgracht 4, T 419 9820).

In the centre, dine alfresco at Singel 404 (Singel 404, T 428 0154), Walem (Keizersgracht 449, T 625 3544) or Brandstof (Marnixstraat 357, T 422 0813). If you're near Bloemenmarkt, head to Café De Jaren (Nieuwe Doelenstraat 20-22, T 625 5771) or, for lunch in a park, 't Blauwe Theehuis (Vondelpark 5, T 662 0254). Café Brecht (Weteringschans 157, T 627 2211) is a popular pitstop before a night of dancing at Jimmy Woo (Korte Leidsedwarsstraat 18, T 626 3150). For holistically pure food, eat at Restaurant As (Prinses Irenestraat 19, T 644 0100), in a former church, or for an equally unconventional setting, try REM Eiland (Haparandadam 45-2, T 688 5501), atop an old oil-rig platform. Alternatively, make your way to Noord, a former industrial zone that now boasts sublime dining at Stork (Gedempt Hamerkanaal 96, T 634 4000). *For full addresses, see Resources.*

Toko MC

Created by local design agency Afarai, Toko MC opened in 2010 in a huge space made intimate by grouped tables and walls swathed in boldly coloured Morse code and DNA-like patterns. Chef Ray Simon's menu reflects the restaurant's initials – Modern Caribbean – and explains the mix of flavours: Jamaican, Trinidadian, Cuban and *Krioyo* (Curaçaoan), as well as Surinamese and Brazilian. Dishes include peanut soup with chicken, spare ribs served with sweet potato and ginger garlic sauce, and Creole-style ceviche of mackerel with grapefruit and avocado. But it's not just food: Toko MC also enlists underground DJs, who keep the mood lively with a playlist that skips from soul and funk to progressive urban beats. *Polonceaukade 5, T 475 0425, www.mconline.nl*

Mazzo

Once a notorious nightclub, these days Mazzo is a renowned trattoria. Concrete Architectural Associates outfitted the space with brickwork, stone and steel, and divided it into a bar and restaurant. Guests dine amid stylised paintings and banquettes, sampling dishes from chef Edwin Hathazi's Italian menu. *Rozengracht 114, T 344 6402, www.mazzoamsterdam.nl*

Restaurant Anna

A further signal that the red-light district is getting a fierce clean-up, this restaurant opened in two monumental 18th-century buildings, connecting gentrifying tourist strip Warmoesstraat with the still fairly 'red' square around Oude Kerk, in 2011. Complete with a terrace and a warm interior of wooden floorboards and copper pendant lamps, the restaurant offers refined European dishes that occasionally embrace the East, such as tuna tartare with black sesame seeds and wasabi cream cheese. Chef Andrès Delpeut was the youngest ever Dutchman to win a Michelin star at his previous endeavour, De Roggebot in Ermelo, and has earned local devotion for his steak served with a chicory salad and cheese croquette. *Warmoesstraat 111, T 428 1111, www.restaurantanna.nl*

Wilde Zwijnen

With a name that translates as 'wild boars', this restaurant is intriguing for its modern Dutch cuisine and its location, in the up-and-coming quarter of Oost. The airy space, cut through with a skylight, has simple wooden tables, hanging plants and distressed brick walls inset with shelves made from drawers salvaged from old wood cabinets. Contrary to the venue's moniker, the menu is dominated less by porcine fare than by locally sourced, organic ingredients, and the cooking methods reflect the district's multi-ethnic population. Dishes here include pork with potato and parsley croquette, fillet of brill with mussels, and to finish, chocolate nutmeg tart with *Haagse hopjes* (Dutch caramel) ice cream. *Javaplein 23, T 463 3043, www.wildezwijnen.com*

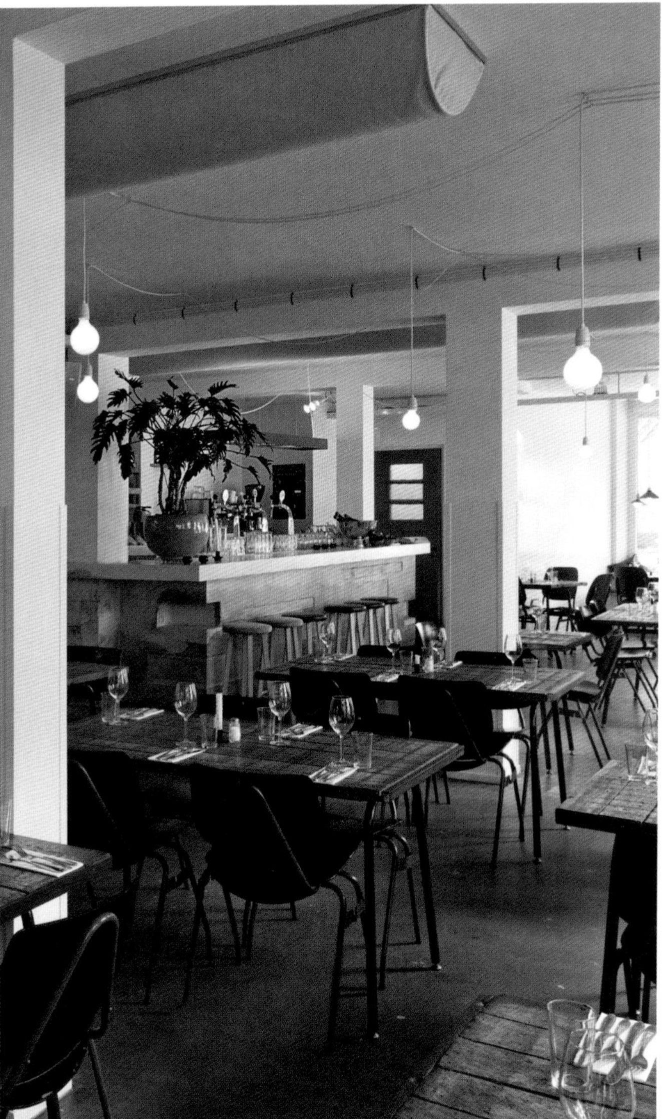

Open

Situated above an old railway bridge, Open affords superb views over the industrial harbour through its floor-to-ceiling windows. The kitchen rustles up French and Italian fare, such as cod and potato fishcakes with blanched celery and aioli, or *tagliatelle nero* with octopus, soft garlic and samphire. Designed by SEVV, the nice mix of ornamental metalwork and custom-printed wallpaper was inspired by the bubbles found in the Bavarian beer that Open serves. On the downstairs wharf there's a tiny outdoor space for dining and drinking. Plans for a jetty are currently being mooted.
Westerdoksplein 20, T 620 1010, www.open.nl

Nel

Whereas many of Amsterdam's eateries spent the first decade of the 21st century being gentrified in a frantic manner, here the owners commissioned a 2009 refurb that resulted in a more relaxed, family-friendly dining experience. This was a smart choice given the building's location, on a square with a playground, overlooking a 17th-century church, canals and the Amstelveld square; all slightly removed from the plethora of sniffy restaurants that clog up nearby Utrechtsestraat. The self-proclaimed owner of 'the most beautiful terrace in Amsterdam' entertains with a menu of pleasing Med-led classic mains and excellent Dutch *hapjes* (bar snacks), including *bitterballen* with mustard. *Amstelveld 12, T 626 1199, www.nelamstelveld.nl*

Nevy
Facing the bold, dramatic futurescape of Noord across the water, this venue packs its own visual punch thanks to all-white fixtures and furniture, and a playfully sinister 'X-ray fish' graphic motif. At plate level, ethically sourced fruits of the sea are served according to instruction (raw, tempura, grilled and so on) by chef Martijn Nijntjes. *Westerdoksdijk 40, T 344 6409*

Lion Noir

There is an *Alice in Wonderland* quality to this French-influenced bar and restaurant. Set in an old coach houseon a busy street, it is elegantly eerie, and crammed with a rotating collection of curiosities that include a dog's skeleton, stuffed birds and a jar containing pickled mushrooms that date back to 1910. The best place to feast on the pan-European menu is from a table in the leafy garden at the rear.

Tuck into seasonal dishes such as Fines de Claire oysters with shallot and red wine vinegar, and black angus steak with duck liver sauce. But the fun begins when chef Edo Kamping, of Bordewijk and Jagershuis fame, fuses Italian fare with Dutch; try his lamb fillet with turnip mash, glazed radish and oyster mushrooms. *Reguliersdwarsstraat 28, T 627 6603, www.lionnoir.nl*

Trouw

Designed by local studio Müller Van Tol, this nightclub's industrial interior is a reminder that the space was once the printworks for some of Holland's leading daily newspapers, including *Trouw*. As a nod to the former occupants, the designers left the huge ventilators and original wall panels, as well as ink stains on the floor of the printing hall. A mounted catwalk connects the club area with the adjacent late-night restaurant, which serves Mediterranean-inspired snacks. Mainly focusing on progressive electronic music, Trouw made its name showcasing international and upcoming bands. Due to an extensive renovation of the area, the venue is due to close in 2014, making a visit to this club that much more urgent. *Wibautstraat 127, T 463 7788, www.trouwamsterdam.nl*

George WPA

A day spent inspecting the art on show in Museumplein could hardly be better rounded off than by checking out the beautiful people in this parkside joint, which was created by the team behind Leidsegracht's Café George (T 626 0802). As in its more central sister, this place strikes just the right balance between casual cool and traditional values, offering a menu of unpretentious brasserie classics such as Caesar salad or leg of duck. As the Waldorf salad indicates, there is a Manhattan twist to this bistro, and when it first opened, locals excitedly compared George WPA to New York's Pastis. There's also George Deli USA, on Utrechtsestraat (T 330 0171), an ideal place for grabbing a buttery croissant and coffee on the go. *Willemsparkweg 74, T 470 2530, www.cafegeorge.nl*

Van Dobben

With its white walls, padded stools and constantly blaring radio, this snack bar evokes Edward Hopper's *Nighthawks*. Pleasingly hidden in a backstreet, well away from the euphemistically titled 'entertainment district' of Rembrandtplein, and within stumbling distance of the fabulous art deco Theater Tuschinski (T 0900 1458), its perennially jolly team of men in white coats serve up a bewildering and ever-changing selection of Dutch culinary favourites. Be sure to try the pea soup (on the menu in winter) and the house speciality – steaming hot breaded croquettes, which are now being stocked in supermarkets throughout the Netherlands. The best part, though, is that everything here is prepared on the spot. *Korte Reguliersdwarsstraat 5, T 624 4200, www.vandobben.nl*

Door74
This sophisticated, low-lit drinking den offers a selective, season-specific menu of gimmick-free cocktails. Owner Sergej Fokke has wilfully defied Amsterdam's famous egalitarian streak by accepting guests via a telephone-only reservation system, although small groups are admitted on the door during the week for a taste of the exclusivity.
Reguliersdwarsstraat 74, T 063 404 5122

De Culinaire Werkplaats

Combining a culinary laboratory, a design
studio and a restaurant under one roof,
Westerpark establishment De Culinaire
Werkplaats is a herbivore's heaven. The
menu is titled 'eatinspirations', which
translates into an ever-changing sequence
of dishes cooked up by the owners,
designer Marjolein Wintjes and chef Eric
Meursing. The bright space, which is
divided into rooms connected by a patio,
is a charming platform for the duo's
ingenious experiments with flowers and
vegetables. Past surprises have included
vegetarian *jus de veau*, marinated turnip
curry and olive-oil cake with black fruit
and liquorice. A fine twist comes at the
end when you ask for the bill, with Wintjes
and Meursing leaving it to guests to
pay what they think the meal is worth.
*Fannius Scholtenstraat 10, T 065 464
6576, www.deculinairewerkplaats.nl*

INSIDERS' GUIDE

CAROLE BAIJINGS AND STEFAN SCHOLTEN, DESIGNERS

The work of design duo Stefan Scholten (opposite, right) and Carole Baijings covers everything from the 'Butte' travel box (see p085), to the reinvention of the MINI One car. Their riverfront studio on the Westerdok affords views over Noord, namely the EYE Film Institute (see p065), to which they often catch the ferry. 'We feel like we're taking a vacation when we get on that boat,' says Baijings. Closer to home, the pair visit photography museum FOAM (see p032) and its nearby shop &FOAM (Vijzelstraat 78, T 760 0489), which specialises in books and magazines.

The couple are regular visitors to Noordermarkt square for its Monday fleamarket, Saturday organic market, and Winkel 43 (Noordermarkt 43, T 623 0223), a café famed for its apple pie and sunny terrace. When in the area, they'll also stop off at florists Pompon (Prinsengracht 8-10, T 622 5137). 'You'll always find its flowers at our openings around the world,' says Baijings. The Nine Streets shopping area (see p072) is highly rated, especially Skins Cosmetics (Runstraat 11, T 528 6922) for its scents. To unwind, the pair enjoy knocking back a traditional *jenever* (Dutch gin) at Wynand Fockink (Pijlsteeg 31, T 639 2695), or ordering a bike-delivered cake from Bakker Baard (Pazzanistraat 11, T 068 191 7218). At night they can be found dancing at Trouw (see p054) or the famed 'pop temple' Paradiso (Weteringschans 6, T 626 4521). *For full addresses, see Resources.*

ARCHITOUR

A GUIDE TO AMSTERDAM'S ICONIC BUILDINGS

Contemporary Dutch architecture is among the most innovative in Europe, but Amsterdam will always have a split personality, its canalside vernacular of gables and large windows contrasting with nonconformist modern buildings. Exciting new projects roll on, including the expansive mixed-use IJDock development at Westerdokseiland; the renovation of the Rijksmuseum (see p032) by Cruz y Ortiz; and the EYE Film Institute (opposite). After flirting with modernist tendencies in the early 20th century through the Amsterdam School, the city decided it was managing nicely with existing traditions, but visitors who venture away from the historic centre may be surprised. In the east, urban development at Het Funen, notably Verdana (Funenpark) by NL Architects, provides evidence of what innovative residential design can look like, and the Zuidas area proves that corporate architecture can have character; remarkable buildings here include the UNStudio Tower (Gustav Mahlerlaan 14). Also noteworthy is the ING Group HQ (Amstelveenseweg 500), designed by Meyer en Van Schooten.

When KNSM, the last of the city's shipping giants, tanked in 1977, Havens Oost was earmarked for reinvention. Unlike most docklands schemes, though, this one was aimed at aesthetes and involved almost every architect in town; the resulting modern interpretation of classic tract housing marked a welcome change. *For full addresses, see Resources.*

EYE Film Institute

Opened in 2012, the new home of the
EYE Film Institute, designed by Delugan
Meissl Associated Architects, resembles
a large white bird about to take flight.
Located in the once forlorn Noord, and
a free two-minute ferry ride from behind
Centraal Station, EYE contains small pods
in which three people at a time can scan
the institute's world-class film collection
or watch a movie from its archives. These
can also be viewed in its four cinemas,
which include an old-Parisian-style
theatre. In addition to the new Tolhuistuin
arts space (T 763 0650), which often
hosts events by Paradiso (see p062) and,
further west, the NDSM (www.ndsm.nl),
a shipyard-turned-creative-complex, there
are now many reasons to cross the IJ.
IJpromenade 1, T 589 1400,
www.eyefilm.nl

Hope, Love and Fortune

Part of the celebrated redevelopment of
the Havens Oost docklands area, Borneo
Sporenburg is largely residential, but
even if you can't wangle an invite to one
of the flats, you must see this 2002 office
and apartment complex designed by
Rudy Uytenhaak. Its Norwegian marble
facade was created in collaboration
with artist Willem Oorebeek.
Rietlandterras 2-54, Borneo Sporenburg

Bijlmer ArenA Station

Located in the city's somewhat neglected
south-east, this train station – finished
in 2007 and designed by UK architects
Grimshaw with Dutch firm Arcadis Bouw/
Infra – links Amsterdam to Utrecht. The
terminus comprises eight elevated tracks,
sheltered by V-shaped steel roofs held
aloft by cantilevered steel arms, and uses
Oregon pine to absorb sound.
Arena Boulevard

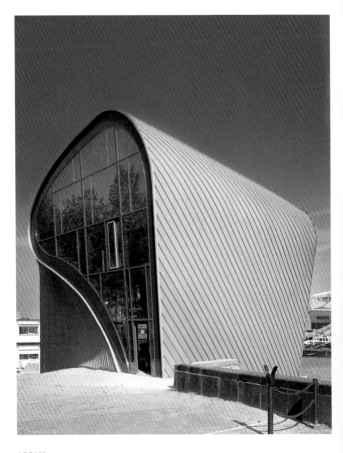

ARCAM

Completed in 2003, and still looking as if it's a vision of some alternate future, the Amsterdam Centre for Architecture, set up in the heart of the city, should be the first stop in any architour of the capital. Intended as a public information point regarding buildings both old and new, it hosts provocative lectures, exhibitions and discussions. We recommend its Archishuttle guides, which give the lowdown on structures of interest according to major tram and bus routes, enabling visitors to see the sights without being herded in with a group of tourists. The waterside HQ, designed by René van Zuuk, also makes a good meeting point. *Prins Hendrikkade 600, T 620 4878, www.arcam.nl*

Openbare Bibliotheek Amsterdam

The Netherlands' largest public library, welcoming some 5,000 visitors daily, Openbare Bibliotheek Amsterdam (OBA), boldly claims to be the hub of the country's cultural life. Located on the Oosterdokseiland, a development east of Centraal Station, the building certainly has the credentials to back up such an assertion, comprising eight massive floors housing everything from the Theater van 't Woord to comic book archives and an exhibition space, Expo Zaal, all connected by an atrium of dizzying proportions. It's all the work of Dutch architect Jo Coenen, whose seventh-floor panorama terrace affords a fabulous vantage point of the city, including Renzo Piano's science centre NEMO (see p012). *Oosterdokskade 143, T 523 0900, www.oba.nl*

SHOPPING

THE BEST RETAIL THERAPY AND WHAT TO BUY

In a city with myriad shops and boutiques – more than 10,000 at the last count – any visitor with a sharp eye is sure to return home laden with loot. Amsterdam's most popular shopping area is undoubtedly The Nine Streets (De Negen Straatjes), which straddle the four main canals. In this quarter, old curiosity shops stand cheek by jowl with boutiques, and you can buy everything from high-end fashion at Rika (Oude Spiegelstraat 9, T 330 1112) to cheeses at De Kaaskamer (Runstraat 7, T 623 3483) and even toothbrushes at De Witte Tanden Winkel (Runstraat 5, T 623 3443); pick up a street map in one of the shops. Nearby thoroughfare Rozengracht is almost entirely dedicated to interiors stores, such as the gleaming Wonen2000 (No 215-217, T 521 8712). For quirky gifts, check out The Otherist (Leliegracht 6, T 320 0420).

Old-school Amsterdammers shop on and around Cornelis Schuytstraat, in Oud Zuid. Here you'll find the flagship of Dutch womenswear label Stills (No 16, T 767 0473) and menswear mecca 1 (see p078). Students and artists furnish their apartments and fill their wardrobes in the gritty but groovy De Pijp area – eco-savvy shoppers hit quirky Charlie + Mary (Gerard Doustraat 84, T 662 8281). And in Havens Oost, cavernous outlets such as Pols Potten (KNSM-Laan 39, T 419 3541) and Keet in Huis (KNSM-Laan 297, T 419 5958) cater mostly to young yuppie families.
For full addresses, see Resources.

United Nude

Galahad Clark, the heir to the British company Clarks, put his best foot forward when he co-founded United Nude with Rem D Koolhaas, the starchitect's nephew and namesake. Long before Marc Jacobs made headlines with his floating heels, the pair were pushing the boundaries of footwear with their own gravity-defying architectural creations, such as the 'Web Hi' shoe (above), €400. Similarly pioneering, their Amsterdam flagship store features jet-black fixtures and large portions of unlit space to direct the gaze unequivocally towards the main event, a curved back wall (overleaf) featuring a giant illuminated grid of towering heels. *Spuistraat 125a, T 330 9796, www.unitednude.com*

Friday Next

Owners Esther Blaffert and Paulien de Vries describe this airy space on the Overtoom as their 'concept store', the concept being, apparently, that they have to really like something before they will stock it. Variously, their passions extend to iconic furniture (Fritz Hansen is well represented, plus the odd 'Thinking Man's Chair' by Jasper Morrison), Royal Republiq bags and the work of Dutch artisan Esther Derkx, whose reconditioned, cast-off crockery is a more original gift than the standard delftware. The small café attached excels at wholesome salads. Altogether, it makes for a charming, refreshingly personal experience on a shopping street that is fast becoming mired in imported identikit interiors.
Overtoom 31, T 612 3292,
www.fridaynext.com

Meeuwig & Zn

Manfred Meeuwig's work as a food stylist, food writer and chef led him to open this Haarlemmerstraat oil store. Disheartened by the popularity of unhealthy pig fat and bland butter as a cooking base among Amsterdam's chef fraternity, this was his way of directing them towards a healthier alternative. The store stocks high-quality olive oils from all over Italy, Spain and France, dispensed from large steel drums, which is not only environmentally commendable (you can take oil away in any old vessel brought from home), but it also means consumers aren't swayed by the niceties of packaging. *Haarlemmerstraat 70, T 626 5286, www.meeuwig.nl*

1

Pronounced *ain*, this has been the go-to store for top-of-the-line, casual menswear and accessories since opening in September 2010. Owner Aebe Ferilli's well-edited collection includes labels such as Strategic Business Unit and Dutch trainer brand Filling Pieces. It's all sold in a warmly lit, masculine environment channelling a rustic New York vibe, featuring painted tin sheets on the walls and raw concrete floors alternating with antique parquet. It's no surprise that the space's uncomplicated style attracts an appreciative local audience, spanning those seeking a nicely cut Barbour coat to cool young hipsters looking for more in the way of edgy basics, such as Orlebar Brown shorts and Tricker's loafers. *Cornelis Schuytstraat 19, T 671 5239, www.1-store.nl*

WonderWood

Wiet Hekking is Amsterdam's sole specialist in vintage plywood designs, and walking into his store is like stepping inside a gallery, except that everything is for sale. Located in the city's historic centre, in a building that boasts one of the oldest painted ceilings in Amsterdam, dating to 1565, WonderWood presents midcentury classics, and new designs. There are re-editions of rare pieces by Ilmari Tapiovaara, Egon Eiermann and Marcel Breuer, as well as newer items, such as Jeroen Wand's 'Slats' chair. Hekking has also introduced an extensive range of beautiful pieces by unknown designers. *Rusland 3, T 625 3738, www.wonderwood.nl*

Tenue de Nîmes

Denim in all shapes and shades is the name of the game at this massive glass-fronted boutique. Owners Menno van Meurs and Rene Strolenberg offer a smart blend of old-school designers and contemporary cult labels such as Momotaro, Acne and Naked & Famous. The contrast in styles is also echoed in the interior, which features a glossy white rear wall, and a backdrop of original 19th-century brickwork, set against which are rows of fluorescent lights that mimic stitching. Alongside the denim are simply cut garments in cotton, silk and wool, bags by Dutch designer Ellen Truijen, and scent from Le Labo and Byredo. You can also buy Japanese washing powder here that conditions denim without bleaching or harming it. *Elandsgracht 60, T 320 4012, www.tenuedenimes.com*

Droog
In a splendid 17th-century building
that was given an exuberant facelift
by French artist Franck Bragigand,
Droog showcases its celebrated designs,
including the 'Sticky Lamp', the 'Bottoms
Up' doorbell, made with wine glasses,
and the 'Milk Bottle Lamp'. Many of the
pieces on sale here are limited editions.
*Staalstraat 7b, T 523 5059,
www.droogdesign.nl*

De Winkel van Nijntje

Holland's most successful living artist isn't an abstract expressionist or a kinetic visionary; it's Dick Bruna, who specialises in hand-drawn depictions of a cute white bunny rabbit. Nijntje (or Miffy, as she's known outside the Netherlands) became a global publishing phenomenon after the first book was released in 1955; her modest adventures, now translated into some 40 languages, have since sold more than 85 million volumes. This store, aptly located in the 'nappy belt' of the smart Rivierenbuurt district, demonstrates just how far Miffy has come as a design icon. As well as the books and bibs you might expect, there are also beautiful pieces of miniature furniture. It is said that Bruna still scrutinises every item.

Scheldestraat 61, T 664 8054,
www.dewinkelvannijntje.nl

The Frozen Fountain

This store's two floors of gallery space showcase well-known design brands such as Driade and Flos, but The Frozen Fountain is principally a hothouse for upcoming and homegrown talent. Piet Hein Eek and Marcel Wanders launched their stellar careers here, so it's hallowed ground for aspiring young Dutch designers. Local crafts are often reinterpreted with a quirky, contemporary twist – check out limited-edition items, which have included the 'Butte' wooden travel box (above), designed by Scholten & Baijings (see p062) in conjunction with the Zuiderzee Museum. It was inspired by 18th-century cases from the northern Netherlands. *Prinsengracht 645, T 622 9375, www.frozenfountain.nl*

Precinct 5
So-called because it used to be a police
station, Precinct 5 plays host to two
complementary stores: Enplus, which
carries everything from APC to Tokyo
label Bedwin & the Heartbreakers; and
a concession for streetwear king Stüssy.
The steel and glass interiors by architects
Kuub offer a suitably masculine backdrop.
Singel 459, T 330 1270,
www.precinct-five.com

SPORTS AND SPAS

WORK OUT, CHILL OUT OR JUST WATCH

When it snows in Amsterdam, the city takes on a magical quality. While tourists admire its winter-wonderland beauty, locals are busy checking the temperature to see if it will drop low enough for long enough to enable them to don their skates. If the big freeze reaches Friesland, then the 200km Elfstedentocht (11 Cities Race) is declared. Weather conditions have only facilitated three in the past 40 years, so most of the time Amsterdammers make do with zooming around the Jaap Edenbaan rink (Radioweg 64, T 694 9652), where skates can be hired from October to March, or Museumplein's reflecting-pool-turned-skating-rink (December to February, 10am-8pm). This obsession continues year-round, as thousands of in-line skaters take to the streets every Friday for a 20km race across town (www.fridaynightskate.com).

Cycling is such a part of Dutch culture that bicycles have right of way; always keep an ear out for them – they're not known as 'the whispering death' for nothing. You can hire one at a MacBike rental (T 624 8391, www.macbike.nl). Meanwhile, De Mirandabad (De Mirandalaan 9, T 252 4444), which has a wave machine and a pebble 'beach', has been usurped as the city's premier swimming venue by the slick, central Het Marnix (Marnixplein 1, T 524 6000). If yoga's more your thing, sign up for a class at the Centrum branch of Bikram Yoga (Korte Prinsengracht 91, T 624 9855).
For full addresses, see Resources.

Klimhal

One of the most popular pastimes for sporty, thrill-seeking Amsterdammers is clambering up this climbing centre's plywood or fibreglass walls, which are studded with multicoloured holds offering different routes and levels of difficulty. Its Lead Climbing Wall is 21m high, and is often used for competitions. Less vertiginous options include Boulderhall, which is carpeted with crash mats, and The Ship; both have a 4m maximum climb. There are also regular one-hour introductory courses, after which you can climb until 10.30pm. *Naritaweg 48, T 681 0121, www.klimhalamsterdam.nl*

Spa Zuiver

A delightful alternative to physical exertion is Spa Zuiver's seemingly endless array of interior and exterior plunge pools and saunas. However, fitness fanatics can still get their fix at the adjoining Hotel Zuiver's impressive gym and indoor tennis facilities. Note: mobile phones are strictly verboten. *Koenenkade 8, T 301 0710, www.spazuiver.com*

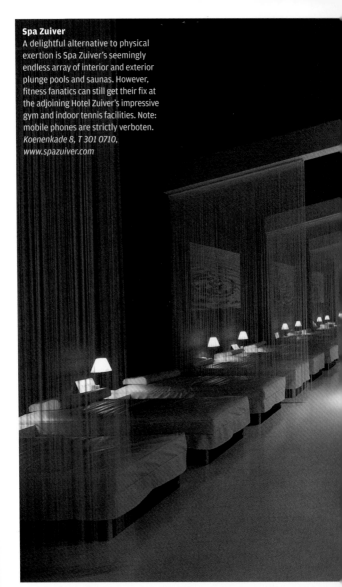

Sento

This luxury spa and health club, situated in a partly transparent box atop the popular Het Marnix swimming pool (see p088), is as Zen as one could hope for in Amsterdam, especially since the Dutch are said to be rather adventurous and earthy. The workout area overlooks the ground-floor pool, where the water is the same level as the canal outside, making it seem as if you're swimming with the ducks on the other side of the glass. There's also an upstairs comfort zone, with rain showers, a jacuzzi (right) and a sauna. Architect Jeroen van Mechelen's use of natural materials and a refined lighting scheme instantly relieve stress. Rock your cares away in one of the swing chairs, and don't forget to enjoy the splendid view from the rooftop terrace. Day passes are available for €22.50.
Marnixplein 1, T 330 1444, www.sento.nl

Amsterdam ArenA
In a city obsessed with its football team,
the 52,000-capacity ArenA stadium, and
Ajax Museum, dedicated to the club's
achievements, is a highlight. Since
the stadium opened in 1996 – the first
in Europe with a sliding roof – more
than a million fans have queued up
for a behind-the-scenes tour. The
Dutch national side also play here.
Arena Boulevard 1, T 311 1333

ESCAPES

WHERE TO GO IF YOU WANT TO LEAVE TOWN

As the Netherlands is such a tiny country (you can drive across it in two hours), a day trip from Amsterdam throws up plenty of options. Art fans should head to The Hague, a 50-minute train ride from Centraal Station, where the yellow-brick Gemeentemuseum (Stadhouderslaan 41, T 070 338 1111), designed by Dutch architect Hendrik Petrus Berlage, boasts a permanent collection of works by Kandinsky, Mondrian, Monet and Picasso. Until mid-2014, the Gemeentemuseum will also be the temporary home of highlights from Mauritshuis (Korte Vijverberg 8, T 070 302 3456), which is undergoing an expansion. This collection majors on masterpieces of the Dutch Golden Age, notably Vermeer's *Girl with a Pearl Earring* (on loan to a Japanese gallery until the Mauritshuis reopens) and *View of Delft*, a haunting portrayal of the artist's hometown, which is a 20-minute tram ride from the city centre.

Haarlem is practically a suburb of Amsterdam, located only 15 minutes by train from Centraal Station, but has a provincial vibe and hip beach clubs in nearby Bloemendaal (opposite). The neighbouring residential city of Almere (see p098) offers a wealth of contemporary architecture. If you want more seclusion, head an hour east from Amsterdam to the five-star De Echoput hotel (Amersfoortseweg 86, T 055 519 1248), near Apeldoorn, set in a beautiful forest and inspired by the work of Frank Lloyd Wright. *For full addresses, see Resources.*

Bloemendaal

Acknowledged as the coolest stretch of coast in the country, Bloemendaal is a hotspot for Amsterdammers in search of sun, sand and sounds. Take the train to Zandvoort, from where it's a 20-minute walk to the beach, or travel to Haarlem, then hop on a bus. From April until September, the beachfront becomes one long lounge-bar-cum-alfresco-nightclub. Head for Republiek (above; T 023 573 0730), or walk down the beach to hippyish hangout Woodstock 69 (T 023 573 2152). For a different vibe, head north to join the surfers at Wijk aan Zee: getting there isn't easy without a car, but taking the half-hourly boat (Fast Flying Ferries, T 0900 266 6399) to Velsen from Centraal Station, with a rented bike for the last stretch, is a great experience. Or follow the hipsters along to Timboektoe (T 025 137 3050).

Almere

Before 1976, Almere didn't exist. Now, sitting on reclaimed land, half an hour's drive from Amsterdam, it is one of the Netherlands' fastest-growing cities. Work began in 1994 on the city centre's raised surface, positioned over parking facilities and bus lanes, and designed by Dutch architects OMA. Almere also boasts the work of Christian de Portzamparc, SANAA, UNStudio and David Chipperfield. SMC Alsop's 16,000 sq m Urban Entertainment Centre, completed in 2003, includes the Apollo Hotel (pictured; T 036 527 4500), with its cedar-clad 'sleeping block' and amorphous brass-clad lobby and public areas. Walk from the station to Weerwater lake and visit the architecture centre Casla (T 036 538 6842), where you can ask for directions to the equally inspiring suburbs of Seizoenenbuurt and Eilandenbuurt.

Suitehotel Posthoorn, Monnickendam

Time holds its breath in Monnickendam, Volendam and Edam. This cluster of traditional fishing villages, only 12km from Amsterdam, is top of the list for the daily buses filled with Japanese and Chinese tourists, who come here to be caught on camera wearing traditional costumes and clogs. But underneath this theme-park craziness is a proud local culture that has managed to retain its identity. Stay at Monnickendam's elegant Posthoorn hotel, which has a private dining room (opposite) and six 17th-century-styled period rooms, such as the Sistermans Suite (above), with its mix of antique and modern furniture, and 17th- and 18th-century paintings. *Noordeinde 43, T 029 965 4598, www.posthoorn.eu*

Cobra Museum, Amstelveen
This suburb, built for wealthy merchants, used to be considered Amsterdam's less racy neighbour. Things started to change, however, when Amstelveen embraced visual art via its impressive Cobra Museum, designed by Wim Quist, which houses key works from the Vrij Beelden, CoBrA and Creatie movements.
Sandbergplein 1-3, T 547 5050, www.cobra-museum.nl

NOTES

SKETCHES AND MEMOS

RESOURCES

CITY GUIDE DIRECTORY

A

1 078
Cornelis Schuytstraat 19
T 671 5239
www.1-store.nl

&FOAM 062
Vijzelstraat 78
T 760 0489
www.foam.nl

Akasha Holistic Wellbeing Center 017
Conservatorium Hotel
Van Baerlestraat 27
T 570 0067
www.conservatoriumhotel.com

Amsterdam ArenA 094
Arena Boulevard 1
T 311 1333
www.amsterdamarena.nl

Amsterdam Roest 040
Czaar Peterstraat 213
T 308 0283
www.amsterdamroest.nl

ARCAM 070
Prins Hendrikkade 600
T 620 4878
www.arcam.nl

B

Bakker Baard 062
Pazzanistraat 11
T 068 191 7218
www.westergasfabriek.nl

Bijlmer ArenA Station 068
Arena Boulevard

Bikram Yoga 088
Korte Prinsengracht 91
T 624 9855
www.bikramyoga.nl

't Blauwe Theehuis 040
Vondelpark 5
T 662 0254
www.blauwetheehuis.nl

Brandstof 040
Marnixstraat 357
T 422 0813

C

Café Brecht 040
Weteringschans 157
T 627 2211
www.cafebrecht.nl

Café George 056
Leidsegracht 84
T 626 0802
www.cafegeorge.nl

Café De Jaren 040
Nieuwe Doelenstraat 20-22
T 625 5771

Casla 098
Weerwaterplein 3
Almere
T 036 538 6842
www.casla.nl

Charlie + Mary 072
Gerard Doustraat 84
T 662 8281
www.charliemary.com

Cobra Museum 102
Sandbergplein 1-3
Amstelveen
T 547 5050
www.cobra-museum.nl

De Culinaire Werkplaats 060
Fannius Scholtenstraat 10
T 065 464 6576
www.deculinairewerkplaats.nl

speakeasy → *reserve a table!*

Dinner
HARBOUR CLUB
* Speak to James

RESTAURANT
RED
- Late night dinner FRIDAY.

HOTELS
ADDRESSES AND ROOM RATES

Amstel 016
Room rates:
double, from €395
Professor Tulpplein 1
T 622 6060
www.amsterdam.intercontinental.com

Apollo Hotel 098
Room rates:
double, from €95
Koetsierbaan 2
Almere
T 036 527 4500
www.apollohotelsresorts.com/almere

Hotel Arena 028
Room rates:
double, from €110;
Studio Room, from €380
's-Gravesandestraat 51
T 850 2400
www.hotelarena.nl

Boat For Rent Amsterdam 016
Room rates:
boat, from €135
(three-night minimum stay)
T 062 190 6630
www.boatforrentamsterdam.com

Canal House 030
Room rates:
double, from €240;
Best Room, from €550
Keizersgracht 148
T 622 5182
www.canalhouse.nl

Citizen M 020
Room rates:
Citizen M room, from €80
Prinses Irenestraat 30
T 811 7090
www.citizenmamsterdamcity.com

The College Hotel 026
Room rates:
double, €205;
Deluxe Room 211, €260
Roelof Hartstraat 1
T 571 1511
www.thecollegehotel.com

Conservatorium Hotel 017
Room rates:
double, from €325;
Conservatorium Suite, €665
Van Baerlestraat 27
T 570 0000
www.conservatoriumhotel.com

The Dylan 023
Room rates:
double, €325;
Loft Suite, €1,650
Keizersgracht 384
T 530 2010
www.dylanamsterdam.com

De Echoput 096
Room rates:
double, €90
Amersfoortseweg 86
Hoog Soeren
T 055 519 1248
www.echoput.nl

Hotel de l'Europe 016
Room rates:
double, €340
Nieuwe Doelenstraat 2-14
T 531 1777
www.leurope.nl

WALLPAPER* CITY GUIDES

Executive Editor
Rachael Moloney

Editor
Ella Marshall
Authors
Jeroen Bergmans
Steve Korver
Alex Onderwater
Mark Smith

Art Director
Loran Stosskopf
Art Editor
Eriko Shimazaki
Designer
Mayumi Hashimoto
Map Illustrator
Russell Bell

Photography Editor
Sophie Corben
Acting Photography Editor
Anika Burgess
Photography Assistant
Nabil Butt

Chief Sub-Editor
Nick Mee
Sub-Editor
Marie Cleland Knowles

Editorial Assistant
Emma Harrison

Wallpaper* Group Editor-in-Chief
Tony Chambers
Publishing Director
Gord Ray
Managing Editor
Jessica Diamond
Acting Managing Editor
Oliver Adamson

Interns
Carmen de Baets
Lillian He
Despina Rangou
Hye-Young Yune

Wallpaper* ® is a
registered trademark
of IPC Media Limited

First published 2006
Second edition (revised
and updated) 2009
Third edition (revised
and updated) 2011
Fourth edition (revised
and updated) 2012

All prices are correct at
the time of going to press,
but are subject to change.

Printed in China

PHAIDON

Phaidon Press Limited
Regent's Wharf
All Saints Street
London N1 9PA

Phaidon Press Inc
180 Varick Street
New York, NY 10014

Phaidon® is a registered
trademark of Phaidon
Press Limited

www.phaidon.com

A CIP Catalogue record for
this book is available from
the British Library.

ISBN 978 0 7148 6445 7

PHOTOGRAPHERS

**Amsterdam Tourism
& Convention Board**
Amsterdam city view,
inside front cover

Joachim Baan
Tenue de Nîmes, p081

Misha de Ridder
NEMO, p012
The Whale, p013
Hope, Love and
Fortune, pp066-067
Klimhal, p089

Arnout Groen
Sento, pp092-093

Eric and Petra Hesmerg
Cobra Museum,
pp102-103

Ewout Huibers
Citizen M, p020, p021
Mazzo, pp042-043

Luuk Kramer
The Exchange, pp024-025
The College Hotel, p026
Canal House, pp030-031
Vlaamsch
Broodhuys, p033
Moooi, p034

Hermitage
Amsterdam, p035
Rabozaal, p036, p037
De Kas, pp038-039
Toko MC, p041
Restaurant Anna,
p044, p045
Wilde Zwijnen, pp046-047
Nel, p049
Lion Noir, p052, p053
Trouw, pp054-055
George WPA, p056
Van Dobben, p057
Door74, pp058-059
De Culinaire
Werkplaats, pp060-061
Carole Baijings and
Stefan Scholten, p063
EYE Film Institute, p065
Openbare Bibliotheek
Amsterdam, p071
United Nude, pp074-075
Friday Next, p076
Meeuwig & Zn, p077
1, pp078-079
De Winkel van Nijntje, p084
Precinct Five, pp086-087
Spa Zuiver, pp090-091

Daniel Nicolas
Droog, pp082-083

Win Ruigrok
ARCAM, p070

Evan Schomaker
Republiek, p097

Inge Vandamme
Hotel V
Frederiksplein, p022
Steel, p027
Open, p048
Bijlmer ArenA
Station, pp068-069
WonderWood, p080

Louis van de Vuurst
Amsterdam ArenA,
pp094-095

AMSTERDAM

A COLOUR-CODED GUIDE TO THE HOT 'HOODS

DE PIJP
This dynamic district boasts a bustling market and fine Amsterdam School housing

WESTERPARK
A gasworks converted into an arts centre has rejuvenated this once rundown area

CENTRUM
Avoid the sleaze and the stag parties, and instead enjoy the upmarket shopping here

JORDAAN
Cool cafés, hip bars and beautiful people inhabit the charming streets of this district

HAVENS OOST
Home to a grandiose docklands regeneration scheme that actually seems to work

OUD ZUID
More than just a museum quarter, the city's first suburb is staging a chic comeback

For a full description of each neighbourhood, see the Introduction.
Featured venues are colour-coded, according to the district in which they are located.